# THE CHRIST CHILD

# THE CHRIST CHILD

## AS TOLD BY MATTHEW AND LUKE

## MADE BY MAUD AND MISKA PETERSHAM

A ZEPHYR BOOK
DOUBLEDAY & COMPANY, INC.
GARDEN CITY, NEW YORK

TO CHRISTIAN EMANUEL

ISBN : 0-385-15841-6
PICTURES COPYRIGHT, 1931
BY MAUD AND MISKA PETERSHAM
ALL RIGHTS OF REPRODUCTION RESERVED
PRINTED IN U.S.A.
9  8  7  6  5  4  3  2

# CONTENTS

1. PROPHECY
2. THE BABE
3. THE SHEPHERDS
4. IN THE TEMPLE
5. THE WISE MEN
6. THE FLIGHT INTO EGYPT
7. THE CHILD

# PROPHECY

For unto us a child is born, unto us a son is given: and the government shall be upon his shoulder: and his name shall be called Wonderful, Counsellor, The mighty God, The everlasting Father, The Prince of Peace. *Isaiah 9:6*

Prepare ye the way of the Lord, make straight in the desert a highway for our God. *Isaiah 40:3*

# THE BABE

And the angel Gabriel was sent from God unto a city of Galilee, named Nazareth, to a virgin espoused to a man whose name was Joseph of the House of David; and the virgin's name was Mary.

And the angel came in unto her and said Hail, thou that art highly favored, the Lord is with thee- blessed art thou among women.

And when she saw him, she was troubled at his saying, and cast in her mind what manner of salutation this should be.

MARY

And the angel said unto her, Fear not, Mary: for thou hast found favour with God. And behold thou shalt bring forth a son and shalt call his name *Jesus.*

He shall be great, and shall be called the Son of the Highest: and the Lord God shall give unto him the throne of his Father David:

And he shall reign over the house of Jacob forever; and of his kingdom there shall be no end.

And it came to pass in those days, that there went out a decree from Caesar Augustus, that all the world should be taxed.

And all went to be taxed, every one into his own city.

And Joseph also went up from Galilee, out of the city of Nazareth, into Judaea, unto the city of David, which is called Bethlehem, to be taxed with Mary his espoused wife, being great with child.

And so it was, that, while they were there, the days were accomplished that she should be delivered.

And she brought forth her firstborn son, and wrapped him in swaddling clothes, and laid him in a manger; because there was no room for them in the inn.

# THE SHEPHERDS

And there were in the same country shepherds abiding in the field, keeping watch over their flock by night.

And, lo, the angel of the Lord came upon them, and the glory of the Lord shone round about them: and they were sore afraid.

And the angel said unto them, Fear not: for behold, I bring you good tidings of great joy, which shall be to all the people.

For unto you is born this day in the city of David a Saviour, which is Christ the Lord.

And this shall be a sign unto you; Ye shall find the babe wrapped in swaddling clothes, lying in a manger.

And suddenly there was with the angel a multitude of the heavenly host praising God, and saying,

Glory to God in the highest, and on earth peace, good will toward men.

And it came to pass, as the angels were gone away from them into heaven, the shepherds said one to another, Let us now go even unto Bethlehem, and see this thing which is come to pass, which the Lord hath made known unto us.

And they came with haste, and found Mary,

and Joseph, and the babe lying in a manger.

And when they had seen it, they made known abroad the saying which was told them concerning this child.

And all they that heard it wondered at those things that were told them by the shepherds.

But Mary kept all these things, and pondered them in her heart.

And the shepherds returned, glorifying and praising God for all the things that they had heard and seen, as it was told unto them.

MARY AND JESUS

# IN THE TEMPLE

# HEROD'S TEMPLE

**A**nd when eight days were accomplished, his name was called Jesus, and they brought him to Jerusalem, to present him to the Lord. And to offer a sacrifice according to that which is said in the law of the Lord. A pair of turtle-doves, or two young pigeons.

And, behold, there was a man in Jerusalem, whose name was Simeon; and the same man was just and devout, waiting for the consolation of Israel: and the Holy Ghost was upon him.

And it was revealed unto him by the Holy Ghost, that he should not see death, before he had seen the Lord's Christ.

And he came by the Spirit into the temple: and when the parents brought in the child Jesus, to do for him after the custom of the law,

SIMEON AND JESUS

Then took he him up in his arms, and blessed God, and said,

Lord, now lettest thou thy servant depart in peace, according to thy word:

For mine eyes have seen thy salvation, which thou hast prepared before the face of all people; A light to lighten the Gentiles and the glory of thy people Israel.

And Joseph and his mother marvelled at those things which were spoken of him.

And Simeon blessed them. And when they had performed all things according to the law of the Lord, they returned into Galilee, to their own city Nazareth.

# THE WISE MEN

Now when Jesus was born in Bethlehem of Judaea in the days of Herod the king, behold there came wise men from the East to Jerusalem, saying,

Where is he that is born King of the Jews? For we have seen his star in the east, and are come to worship him.

When Herod the king had heard these things, he was troubled, and all Jerusalem with him.

And when he had gathered all the chief priests and scribes of the people together, he demanded of them where Christ should be born.

And they said unto him, In Bethlehem of Judaea; for thus it is written by the prophet.

And thou, Bethlehem, in the land of Juda, art not the least among the princes of Juda: for out of thee shall come a Governor, that shall rule my people Israel.

Then Herod, when he had privily called the wise men, enquired of them diligently what time the star appeared.

And he sent them to Bethlehem, and said, Go and search diligently for the young child; and when ye have found him, bring me word again, that I may come and worship him also.

When they had heard the king, they departed; and lo, the star, which they saw in the east, went before them, till it came and stood over where the young child was.

When they saw the star, they rejoiced with exceeding great joy.

And when they were come into the house, they
saw the young child with Mary his mother, and fell

down, and worshipped him: and when they had opened their treasures, they presented unto him gifts; gold, and frankincense and myrrh.

And being warned of God in a dream that they should not return to Herod, they departed into their own country another way.

# THE FLIGHT INTO EGYPT

And when the wise men were departed, behold, the angel of the Lord appeareth to Joseph in a dream, saying, Arise, and take the young child and his mother, and flee into Egypt, and be thou there until I bring thee word: for Herod will seek the young child to destroy him.

When he arose, he took the young child and his mother by night, and departed into Egypt: and was there until the death of Herod: that it might be fulfilled which was spoken of the Lord by the prophet, saying, Out of Egypt have I called my son.

But when Herod was dead, behold, the angel of the Lord appeareth in a dream to Joseph in Egypt, saying: Arise and take the young child and his mother, and go into the land of Israel: for they are dead which sought the young child's life.

And they came and dwelt in a city called Nazareth: that it might be fulfilled which was spoken by the prophets, He shall be called a Nazarene.

# THE CHILD

And the child grew, and waxed strong in spirit, filled with wisdom: and the grace of God was upon him.

Now his parents went to Jerusalem every year at the feast of the passover.

And when he was twelve years old, they went up to Jerusalem after the custom of the feast.

And when they had fulfilled the days, as they returned, the child Jesus tarried behind in Jerusalem; and Joseph and his mother knew not of it.

But they, supposing him to have been in the company, went a day's journey; and they sought him among their kinsfolk and acquaintance.

And when they found him not, they turned back again to Jerusalem, seeking him.

And it came to pass, that after three days they found him in the temple, sitting in the midst of

the doctors, both hearing them, and asking them

questions.

And all that heard him were astonished at his understanding and answers.

And when they saw him, they were amazed: and his mother said unto him, Son, why hast thou thus dealt with us? Behold, thy father and I sought thee sorrowing.

And he said unto them, How is it that ye sought me? Wist ye not that I must be about my Father's business?

And they understood not the saying which he spake unto them.

And he went down with them, and came to Nazareth, and was subject unto them: but his mother kept all these sayings in her heart.

And Jesus increased in wisdom and stature, and in favour with God and man.